The Way of Eden

The Way of Eden

Resisting the Darkness

Jonathan Dillon

RESOURCE *Publications* • Eugene, Oregon

THE WAY OF EDEN
Resisting the Darkness

Copyright © 2025 Jonathan Dillon. All rights reserved. Except for brief quotations in critical publications or reviews, no part of this book may be reproduced in any manner without prior written permission from the publisher. Write: Permissions, Wipf and Stock Publishers, 199 W. 8th Ave., Suite 3, Eugene, OR 97401.

Resource Publications
An Imprint of Wipf and Stock Publishers
199 W. 8th Ave., Suite 3
Eugene, OR 97401

www.wipfandstock.com

PAPERBACK ISBN: 979-8-3852-6479-7
HARDCOVER ISBN: 979-8-3852-6480-3
EBOOK ISBN: 979-8-3852-6481-0
VERSION NUMBER 11/24/25

Scripture quotations are from The Holy Bible, English Standard Version (ESV®), Copyright © 2001 by Crossway, a publishing ministry of Good News Publishers. Used by permission. All rights reserved.

For my Sons

Contents

Introduction | ix

Chapter 1: World without End | 1
Chapter 2: The Way of Babylon | 6
Chapter 3: Pockets of Eden | 11
Chapter 4: Gardeners in Exile | 16
Chapter 5: The Resistance of a Peaceful People | 23
Chapter 6: Dominion or Dominance? | 29
Chapter 7: Songs of Exile | 34
Chapter 8: The Garden of Sorrow | 39
Chapter 9: Trees Planted by Streams of Water | 43
Chapter 10: Music in the Trees | 48

Bibliography | 53

Introduction

MY SOUL WAS SHAPED by mountains. The ancient, story-soaked slopes of Appalachia will always be not simply the home of my youth, but a force carving both my imagination and the way I experience the world around me. Its swift-flowing streams tumbling down from hidden springs have always called me "further up and further in."[1] The rhythm of coal trains singing out of the hollows, the food spread out on the tables of country churches, the rich wordplay of its storytellers, all these have shaped me.

Appalachia is not a place of constant sunshine and joy, though it has these in abundance; deep shadow and sorrow are at home here. The slopes covered in rhododendron and mountain laurel, shady valleys where the sun is a rare visitor, and introspection and contemplation are as natural as the ferns which blanket the forest floor.

The music and the stories of its people bear the battle scars of the violence, poverty, and prejudice that have twisted their way into the mountains like poison ivy snaking its way up the trunks of mountain oaks. The ivy may have covered their trunks, yet oak branches still reach for the sun. A story of victory in the face of adversity and the power of longing and hope written in soil and leaves.

My own childhood was a blessing; loving parents raised my siblings and me in a book-filled home, where laughter and

---

1. Lewis, *The Last Battle*, 196.

Introduction

Scripture were fixtures of life. Yet even in the Garden of Eden, a serpent lurked in the trees. For me, that serpent was named depression, and I have heard its whispers all my life.

I have never vanquished it or been able to simply leave it behind. It follows me like a hound in the dark, and despite the well-meaning bits of advice sweet-hearted folks have offered, I feel its presence still. 'Just cheer up,' as though it was a switch to be flipped on and off. Like a patient with a deep cut, willpower alone will not stop the bleeding. It must be cleaned, bound, and protected so that time and nature can stitch it closed. Once the wound heals, blood will no longer pour out, but there will be scars left to mark the experience.

I have never cured my depression. I fight it. At times, I have pushed it far away, but the battle always continues. Discussing it as something to be cured has simply never described the way I experience depression. It requires constant warfare, purposeful acts of resistance, and being fully aware that the Lord is with me; my foe cannot drive him from my side.

Should the Lord wish it, I do not doubt depression would flee. Indeed, I long for the day when, safe in the mountains of the world to come, it will not darken my mind. But I am not yet removed from the front lines. The battle rages around me, and I must hold my ground. The way Scripture describes our struggle against evil and the effects of sin resonates deep within my heart. The fiery darts of the wicked one are not simply something to be endured, but something to be resisted. I raise the shield of faith and face the foe.

As a young man, I found the ritual of fly-fishing to be a powerful weapon to wield. Slipping silently through the woods, I was drawn to the dark pools where the beauty of a watery world waited to be discovered. The jewel-like colors of the rainbow trout and the hypnotic green maze of a brook trout's back are, to me, like echoes of the Kingdom of Heaven, expressions of his beauty and creativity. The act of casting a tiny hook into the water's current, hoping to touch a world to which I was a stranger, narrowed the worries of life to a simple act of hope and joy. I know of no one who prays

Introduction

with the passion and focus as a fisherman who sees a trout rise to inspect his fly as it sits perched upon the water.

To struggle with depression is not a passive thing, though it may appear to be so. Walking the dog when I want to sit and sulk, getting out of bed and brewing coffee, countless other small tasks can become purposeful acts of resistance to an enemy that seeks to bind me in chains of sorrow, fear, paranoia, and immobility. They become acts of worship and loyalty as I seek to honor my king and resist the fire of the enemy. Others I have spoken to avoid their worries through constant busyness and puttering; in order to fight the foe, they force themselves to rest, to lie down in green pastures. The actions seem to be unalike but are in reality twins. There is no one-size-fits-all, no cookie-cutter method with guaranteed results, just a calling to resist the enemy. To image God in a world that is twisted and broken.

I do not believe this technique of intentional acts of resistance to be unique to those who struggle with depression, but applies to all those who fight against the Kingdom of Darkness. It is the motive behind fasting, the rhythm of communion, and the poetry of baptism. Not a magic spell that banishes problems, but acts of war against an enemy who will not leave us alone.

We are a generation who delights in grand gestures and quick results, but there is a power in longing, in faithful hope. A power as old as the Garden of Eden.

Chapter 1

World without End

ONCE LONG AGO, WHEN the trees were young and sorrow had not yet found a home in the hearts of men, there grew a garden. This was no mere patch of vegetables nor an elegant tree-lined path, but a temple, a meeting place where God walked with man in the cool of the day. A place of such beauty and mystery that even in the glaring lights of modernity, its memory haunts our steps.

High upon the mountain of God, whether in this world or a doorway between the physical creation and the spiritual heavens I do not know, but it was there that God carried Adam and there that Eve awoke. They walked not in idle self-indulgence but were raised by the will of the Maker to work and keep the garden. They were to have dominion over it and all the creatures of this world. Made to be the image of God, made to represent the ways of the Kingdom that was, and is, and is yet to come.

We call the garden Eden, an ancient word meaning delight, and so it was. Beautiful and practical, a place of purpose and abundance. A strange balance in our world, one which even the church seems to have lost. For beauty has been relegated to frivolity, like a limb severed on a battlefield. Either we walk in open worship of utilitarian dreams, or else we abandon hard work and the responsibilities we were created to carry. Pursuing beauty with a gluttonous appetite never satiated, we are incapable of any loyalty save to the goddess Novelty.

Has the garden ever been farther away than it feels today? I do not know, but it feels so very far away. Can we have a conversation? You and I? Is it possible to even hear one another over the rattling spears of keyboard battles and the protest lines of modern tribalism? I hope so, and in that hope, I write to you, Christian, longing to know that I am not alone and that my words can reach you.

Banished from Eden we may be, but the longing for it grows stronger the darker our world becomes. Truly it is not Eden's beauty our souls are reaching for; beauty and natural wonder we have in abundance. It is that there, we were at home. God walked with us, and all was as it should be. There was a wholeness about it, a rightness that we long for. Both the saved and the lost sense that something is terribly wrong. The shadows and distractions our world offers us will not lend hope to the exile. Our souls were made for the Kingdom of God. Augustine was right: we will always be restless till we rest in Him.[1]

Yes, the garden lies behind us, but it also lies ahead of us.

> "Then the angel showed me the river of the water of life, bright as crystal, flowing from the throne of God and of the Lamb through the middle of the street of the city; also, on either side of the river, the tree of life with its twelve kinds of fruit, yielding its fruit each month. The leaves of the tree were for the healing of the nations. No longer will there be anything accursed, but the throne of God and of the Lamb will be in it, and his servants will worship him."[2]

Joy unspeakable and full of glory, healing for the nations? Please, God, hasten the day. In Eden the trees were a testing, but one day, all the branches will hold hope and healing, and while that day gleams bright on the horizon, the light of God's forgiveness is with us today. On the tree of Calvary, God himself has made right

---

1. Augustine, *Confessions*, 3.
2. Revelation 22:1–3.

our failure and called to us to come and follow him. The hope of Christ lies behind us and before us, but we also walk in it today.

> "Even though I walk through the valley of the shadow of death, I will fear no evil, for you are with me; your rod and your staff, they comfort me. You prepare a table before me in the presence of my enemies; you anoint my head with oil; my cup overflows. Surely goodness and mercy shall follow me all the days of my life, and I shall dwell in the house of the Lord forever."[3]

Verses such as the 23rd Psalm have a comforting effect. We have read them so often that we no longer hear the war cry locked in their words. "I will not walk in fear of you, Death, for the Shepherd is with me." The enemies of God will look on in defeat as Christ prepares for us a banquet in their presence.

What a strange thing to do. When the host of darkness assembles against us, Christ prepares a table. When Eve took from the forbidden tree, was she not surrounded by all the trees of Eden? They were all for her, their boughs groaning beneath the abundance of God's grace. Yet she had eyes only for one tree and the dark promises whispered from its branches; whispers which linger in our homes and churches. Whispers of another way. Why should heaven make the rules? Why should our own wisdom not set the pattern? The voice of the Dark does not present itself as a fool or as a foe, but with half-truths and twisted virtue, it lures us farther from the way of the Garden and the God who breathed into us the breath of life.

Let us not be blind to its power; we see it all around us. The pages of history drip red with its lies. It preaches another way, the Way of Babylon. We sit like dragons, coiled and ready to strike, on the treasures God has entrusted us to steward. The wonder of creation has become nothing but resources to be burned in the factories of our own lust, and the people, those imagers of God, are seen as threats to our own hoards. With snarling lips and grudging hearts,

---

3. Psalm 23:4–6.

we offer charity to those beneath us. We have broken our covenant; we live in a world made in the image of our own twisted hearts.

The church has struggled against the Way of Babylon since ancient times, and while the truths of God's Word do not change, our enemy does not sit still. He twists like a serpent, changing the angle of attack, but his goals remain the same: not to turn you into the greatest of sinners but simply to cause you to wander from your calling, to abandon your post. He hopes to blind you to the Garden and focus your eyes on the forbidden. Stripping the contentment and peace from your life, leaving you in headlong pursuit of treasures made of shadow and unmoved by the beauty and purpose of the Kingdom of God. "An ever-increasing craving for an ever-diminishing pleasure."[4]

The people of Christ must hold their ground, firm in the revealed words of God, but light on their feet, wise as serpents and gentle as doves. Yet too often it is difficult to distinguish the church from a corporation. The tactics of the boardroom replace fasting and prayer; marketing instead of friendship; growth instead of community.

To be the church is not a defensive calling; it is an offensive move against the very gates of Hell itself. But how? That is the question for which I write this book. This is a book about resistance, about vision, about a return to the values of the Garden, to the sermons of Christ. It is about something I will call the Greenway, in memory of the Garden.

QUESTIONS FOR REFLECTION

1. Does thinking of Eden as more than just a garden change the way you view the creation story?
2. In Genesis, Adam and Eve are called to "work and keep" the Garden. What does this suggest about humanity's original purpose?

---

4. Lewis, *The Screwtape Letters*, 44.

3. Why do you think Psalm 23 is described not just as comforting, but as a war cry?
4. How do the voices of the serpent still echo in today's culture and church life?
5. How does the author connect the Garden of Eden to the Cross of Calvary and the Tree of Life?

Chapter 2

The Way of Babylon

BEHIND THE BENT DEEDS of mankind twists a serpent, a representation of powers fallen from glory, intent on carving kingdoms and power for themselves. Rebels who have forsaken their king, they seek to sway the children of Adam like wheat in a field. Prowling like beasts in the darkness, they walk unseen, but their presence is felt.

To assume that Cain was the only one for whom sin was "crouching at the door"[1] is naive; the Dark seeks to dominate you as well. Scripture warns of its influence and speaks of its desires in many ways. Perhaps the most striking warning is through the imagery of Babylon. In Scripture, it becomes shorthand for the rejection of the Kingdom of God, representing instead a kingdom of sin.

In the twilight of the kingdom of Judah marched Nebuchadnezzar, king of Babylon, bringing fire and fury to Jerusalem. The Temple was torn down, its treasures plundered, its priests enslaved, while princes and commoners alike were deported from their homes and sent into exile in Babylon.

The paganism and violence of the city caused it to become a symbol for all that is opposed to the Kingdom of Heaven. It was

1. Genesis 4:7.

an anti-Eden, a beautiful garden city dedicated to the darkness. At times, the Bible is referring to the ancient city of Babylon, and sometimes it is discussing more than just the physical reality.

The prophet Isaiah, in the fourteenth chapter of his book, appears to be speaking against the king of Babylon, when suddenly, in verse 12, he seamlessly moves to addressing Satan, the serpent of the garden. He speaks as if Satan is the real king of Babylon, a shadowy power lurking behind the physical throne.

The Apostle Paul warns the church of this unseen threat in his letter to the Ephesians. Our enemy is not flesh and blood, but principalities and powers, the rulers of the darkness of this world, spiritual wickedness in the heavenly places.[2] Unseen but real, intelligent, organized spiritual beings at war with Heaven and its king. This is Babylon. Truly, our enemies are not men and women, but the spiritual beings who manipulate the world around us. Racism and bigotry have no place in the Christian life; our struggle is not against the hostages but the spiritual foes who hold them captive. Let us never waver in our love for all peoples and our desire to see salvation for the nations.

The King James retains the older word "principalities," the princes of the darkness. Unlike modern fairy tales, a prince was not a way of referring only to a ruler in training, eagerly pursuing romances, but suggests the whole concept of royalty and authority. A king or master, a general, or a statesman; all could be called princes because the meaning behind the word implied power. Here is the reality behind the words: there is a war raging around us, and we cannot serve two masters. The armies of Babylon burned Jerusalem and its holy temple, and ever after, it has become a symbol for the supernatural kingdom of Satan that rejoiced in its flames.

The ancient Hebrews seldom reference demonic or evil spiritual powers in the terms that modern Christians are comfortable with. Though it may be inconvenient, it is not their place to speak our language; instead, in our studies, we seek to understand them. While our modern cultures would establish a term and stick to it, creating a catalog of interrelated sets, biblical Hebrew uses word

---

2. Ephesians 6:12.

pictures and visual concepts. For instance, evil spiritual beings are often described as animals of the night or the wilderness[3]

Perhaps this seems strange to you, sitting comfortably in your home, but let us for a moment imagine that we have left home behind and find ourselves traveling the wilderness of the ancient world in a caravan moving from well to well, fully aware of the dangers of the road. As night falls, our group sets up camp, building a fire and turning our eyes to the flames and our backs to the darkness. As the campsite settles, noises in the night capture your attention. Is that the tread of a lion? Is that the laughter of a jackal or of a witch? Unseen creatures prowl the shadows, and your imagination will do the rest. This unease gave birth to the symbolic way of talking about the demonic. The creatures of Babylon, fallen watchers, animal-like in their ferocity, are connected in Scripture to the creatures of the wilderness. Creatures who devour and defile.

When our Lord set out to confront Satan, he did so in the wilderness, and is there a setting more fitting for God to confront Satan than in an un-garden?[4] There among the rocks of the Judean hills, Satan tempted Christ, trying to lure him into following the Way of Babylon, into becoming like him.

Satan tried and tried again, his cunning defeated by Christ's faithfulness. Frustrated, he made an offer: worship me, and I will give you all the kingdoms of this world.[5] Here, the motive of our foe is stripped of its cover. He considers the nations his to do with as he pleases; even Paul refers to Satan as the "god of this world".[6] The phrase goes off like a gunshot, but Paul is not teaching polytheism. There is only one God, but He created many spiritual beings, some of whom have rebelled and desire to be worshipped as deities. Stealing what rightfully belongs to the King, this world is "enemy-occupied territory,"[7] and we are indeed behind enemy lines.

3. Isaiah 13:19-22, Jeremiah 50:39-40, Revelation 18:2-3.
4. Matthew 4:1.
5. Matthew 4:8-9.
6. 2 Corinthians 4:4.
7. Lewis, *Mere Christianity*, 46.

The Way of Babylon

The serpent may twist and thrash, but he is no god like our God; he is a liar and the father of lies. The world does, however, offer him its loyalty, charting the courses of their lives by the values of his kingdom, by the Way of Babylon. They may offer him their devotion, but as Jesus said so beautifully, you shall worship the Lord your God, and him only shall you serve.[8]

Our goal was made clear to us by the Holy Spirit: resist the devil, and he will flee from you.[9] The question we are left with is how? Are we all to become monks, dedicated to silence and prayer? Are we all to separate completely from the world around us, leaving the lost in the clutches of the Dark? Are church attendance, Bible reading, and giving to charity enough to check the advance of Babylon?

Are only the wealthy and powerful able to make a difference? Is it all about grand gestures and sinless perfectionism, or can God use even small and broken creatures like me? It feels like I should have the ability to make a difference, to bring battle to Hell's gates, but how can I make a difference in a battle which has been swirling since nearly the dawn of time?

Not by yourself; the Lord is with you. The God who brought beauty out of chaos and caused the blossoms of Eden to spring up, that same God stands by you as you face the chaos of the modern world. We wander beyond the gates of the garden, but we do not sit idle in the shadows. We must garden; we must cultivate love, joy, peace, patience, kindness, goodness, faithfulness, gentleness, and self-control; these are the fruits of the Spirit.[10] We resist the twisted message of Babylon, not by becoming like it, but by imaging our Lord.

---

8. Matthew 4:10.
9. James 4:7.
10. Galatians 5:22.

QUESTIONS FOR REFLECTION

1. How does recognizing that we wrestle against spiritual powers (not people) reshape the way we view cultural, political, or social conflicts today?

2. Where do you see evidence of the "Way of Babylon" in modern life?

3. How can the church resist the influence of Babylon while still engaging the world around us?

4. Do you ever feel powerless in the spiritual struggle? What practices (prayer, Scripture, fasting, service) help strengthen you to resist it's power?

5. The chapter asks: "Can God use even small and broken creatures like me?"—How would you answer that for yourself?

Chapter 3

Pockets of Eden

TIMES ARE HARD, AND the night is dark. The vast, sweeping emptiness spreads from horizon to horizon, but it is not the emptiness that catches my eye. I see the stars. Silvery dancers walking in a stately procession older than the fears of man. I am aware of what they are, but from where I sit looking up into the night, they seem much more. They are like holes in the fabric of reality through which the lights of another world peek through; like notes of music I cannot understand. They call my mind to wonder.

The darkness of Babylon may stretch through time and space, its twisted hands grasping generation after generation, but even a spot of light in the darkness is enough to turn our eyes towards heaven. Babylon is strong, but it can be resisted, for the Lord is with us. The church is not just a gathering of forgiven sinners; we are the temple of the living God. His power and presence dwell in those who bear his image. In the simplicity of starlight, we can hear the call of the horns of Heaven, the drums of the Lord of Hosts calling his people to battle. Yes, one day the skies will open, and our Lord will come again, but until then, we wage war against the darkness.

The weapons of our war are not those of this world, not violence, hatred, isolation, and self-obsession, but quiet, steady light.

Every moment when temptation is resisted is a blow struck against Babylon; every purposeful act of worship, every moment of faithfulness, proclaims that Christ is King, and we are his.

God has equipped his church to combat the emptiness of Babylon, but not with the weapons you might expect. Just as darkness is an absence of light, so sin is an absence of righteousness. To resist it, we must be as the stars, lights in the darkness. To be what God intended us to be all along, we must wield love, joy, peace, patience, gentleness, goodness, and self-control.

Deep in the coal fields of Appalachia, an old woman moved silently by lantern light through the twisted trees of the mountains. Secrecy was the order of the day, for the heavy hands of the coal company gun thugs allowed no one to stir waves in the great pools of their wealth. Mother Jones, she was called, and she preached unionism, noncompliance, and ultimately violence to shake the hold of oppression and racism that held the people of West Virginia's hollows bound to the wheels of profit.[1] She exhorted the average man and woman to stand up and make a difference. Regardless of her politics and methods, surely the imagery of an old woman risking life and limb to battle forces far greater than herself is inspiring. Before you and me lies a far greater foe and a battle much older and wider in its scope. Though the church may feel it is besieged, our calling is not to fortify our position but to advance upon Hell's gates.[2]

We have embraced a model of a church that is reliant on stages and professionals; celebrity and wealth seem to drive our movement, but though our feet are moving quickly, we don't seem to be making much progress. Bigger buildings and better concerts cannot replace discipleship and Scripture. I am not opposed to lovely buildings nor the beauty of collective effort. Indeed, we don't have enough of them, but our constructions are often soulless, reminding the visitor more of a hotel conference room than a place designed to aid the soul to reach for God. Attendance, I fear, has replaced discipleship, and rather than seeking ways to bring

---

1. Green, *The Devil Is Here in These Hills*, 43, 91.
2. Matthew 16:18.

war to the enemy, we have been lulled into a defensive mindset. It is as though we think that if we have a good crowd and a healthy budget, all must be well. Does your very soul not cry out that all is not well? That there is a rot in our garden? More of the same, just bigger and better, is not the answer.

The church is not designed to fit into this world, and when we begin to find ourselves at ease in Babylon, we should examine our priorities. In the vision of the Western church, something is bent if not broken. We must re-examine if we are truly making disciples; are we really trying our best? If the sins of our fathers are apparent to us through the lenses of hindsight, can we really be so blind to the present?

The roaring voice of Babylon has deafened the ears of many. If we are to be heard, we must not harmonize with its song. Any visitor to our services would be excused for thinking that we draw our inspiration from concerts rather than from Scripture, and that our teachers are the students of politicians rather than the prophets. In short, we are in a funk. Teachers itch to be thought original, and casting aside the voices of the generations before us, they set out seeking new revelations, pursuing the word *viral* rather than *faithful*. Indeed, many of our leaders have no understanding of our Christian past at all, instead relying on the caricatures of revisionist history and resurrecting old heresies long thought dead.

The pews of the Church have become a dangerous place to be. Not that it hasn't always been so; the good old days weren't all that good, for Satan has always sought to kill, silence, or confuse mankind. Yet, there is a heaviness to the darkness now; vices long forced to hide in the shadows of society walk openly. People are as divided now as they have ever been. It feels like the enemy is growing stronger, and rather than cause us to hide or despair, it should stir us to action, clarity, and compassion. It should spur us to hide God's words in our hearts, to meditate, fast, and pray. We should feel the need to come to the table of communion, and to stand proudly in the waters of baptism, for we are standing against the foe, and the Spirit of God dwells within us.

Our enemy is not our fellow man; it is not sinners, but the ruler of the darkness of this world. Satan walks about as a roaring lion seeking whom he may devour.[3] So let us shine light into the darkness. Let us show the angry, disappointed masses that in the garden of God yet grow the fruits of the Spirit. These will attract attention, for they are not native to Babylon, and the hearts of all the children of Adam crave them.

Our hands have been trained to fight, but have our hearts been taught to serve? Is there still a gardener in the heart of man? For that is what we were made to be, priests of the garden. If Babylon's way is one of death, the Lord's way is one of life. Cast your mind back to the stories of the Gospels; wherever our Lord walked, pockets of Eden exploded around Him. Death and sickness vanished at his voice; demonic powers fled from his presence; the wilderness overflowed with food to feed the hungry, and even water turned to wine at the sight of his face. He sought out the broken and brought hope and beauty back into their lives.

If we cannot raise the dead, let us comfort the grieving; if we cannot multiply the loaves and the fish, let us heat up our ovens and feed them the old-fashioned way. The miraculous occurs when the Lord wills it, but He has given you hands to work, eyes to see, and ears to hear. Use what strength you have to show the image of God. If the organized church around you refuses to stop imaging Babylon, then your choice to walk a different path will stand out all the more.

Christian, you can make a difference in this world. Your voice matters so much; not just because of your amazing talents but because the Lord is with you. He is calling you to walk the same road he did. Forsaking the tools of Babylon, reach for our Savior. The task may be too great for me, but it is not too great for my King. I will plant the seeds, but God gives the increase.[4] This has always been the way of the gardener, just as Adam once tended the garden. So let us wield what strength we have and join in the calling

---

3. I Peter 5:8.
4. I Corinthians 3:6–7.

God has placed upon us. Let us till our plot of life and look with eagerness for the coming of the King.

QUESTIONS FOR REFLECTION

1. How can you purposefully embody the fruits of the Spirit in a way that actively resists Babylon's values?
2. What ordinary acts of service could you practice this week to reflect being "pockets of Eden"?
3. How can your church shift from attendance-driven models toward intentional discipleship and community?
4. What practices help guard your heart from being "at ease in Babylon"?
5. How does remembering that "we plant the seeds, but God gives the increase" shape your approach to ministry or daily faithfulness?

Chapter 4

Gardeners in Exile

IN SEPTEMBER 1931, THREE friends argued beneath the swaying yew trees of Addison's Walk, a leafy path on the campus of Magdalen College in Oxford. Veterans of the first World War, they had endured the killing fields of France. Never before had the grist mill of war ground so many lives into dust, and those that lived through it bore the mental scars of a world ended.

In the echo of the cruel reality of the trenches and their aftermath, these men were struggling to put into words how they saw the world around them. Had the guns of the front banished all beauty from their minds? Was there even a place for poetry, stories, and metaphysical truth in the fluorescent lights of the dawning modern world? Perhaps life should be boiled down into simple scientific facts and the empty pursuit of "eat, drink, and be merry for tomorrow we die"?[1] Is the scientific explanation of "how" a replacement for the spiritual question of "why", or can both coexist even in the brutal shadow of a modern war?

The crushed stone path crunched beneath the treading feet of C.S. Lewis, J.R.R. Tolkien, and Hugo Dyson, and while the chill of evening crept into the air and the stars began one by one to take

---

1. 1 Corinthians 15:32.

their places in the sky, they discussed the role of stories, myths, and religion.

As they walked the looping path, Lewis put forth his assertion that religion, myths, and stories are lies, beautiful, but lies nonetheless. His friends strongly disagreed. Inspired by their Christian faith, they insisted that describing what a thing is made of hardly describes the reality of the thing itself, and that just because a story is ancient doesn't mean that it's a lie. A description of the cellular composition of two human beings fails to encompass the reality of two lovers or a mother and her child. A biological exploration of the make-up of trees will hardly suffice to describe the experience of leaves falling in the autumn wind. We do not experience the world around us as a collection of facts; it, and we too, are more than that. The wonder of science and its quest to reveal the hidden truths of what a thing is will always fall short of expressing the thing itself. It may count the brush strokes, but it cannot capture the art of a painting. It is true that humans are composed of cells, but that it is not enough to express the reality of humanity, or even of a tree.

The spirit of the age may seek to wipe wonder and beauty from the earth, and well it might try, for both are expressions of God's nature. But mankind was made for more than brute facts. A simple roof may be enough to keep off the rain, but every culture produced by the world has sought to create more than mere function. We were made to image God, and he is beautiful. Our ideas of what is beautiful will differ, but not our knowledge that life is better when we strive for higher things. There is something in us that rejoices in their presence.

Tolkien would go on to write a poem summarizing his argument against Lewis's claims that evening, a poem he titled *Mythopoeia*, and in my opinion, he captures Christianity's message of resistance to the darkness of Babylon and the meaninglessness of modernity's prophets. Claiming not that evil does not exist or that its power is not overwhelming, he writes that we were made to resist it, poetically showing the heroic struggle of faithfulness.[2]

---

2. Zaleski and Zaleski, *The Fellowship*, 188.

The Way of Eden

I may not have the power to turn the shadow of Babylon aside, but I do have the power to resist, to strike a blow, even if it is a small one. Small stones have felled giants before. Modernity may once have lulled people to sit contented in the lie that good and evil do not exist, but I cannot believe this farce will last forever. The oppression of the weak, the violence of our cultures, the abuse, the excuses—does not your very soul cry out against these things? Whether you lean left or right, do you not feel the weight of the iron crown of Babylon seeking to grind you down, urging you to just accept things, telling you that you don't matter? That there is no point to struggling against the way things are? We know something needs to be done; we just feel unequal to the task. Or we mistake our brothers and sisters as the true enemy, while an unseen evil manipulates, hypnotizes, and imposes itself on humanity.

In the ancient world, a different war left the lives of God's people shattered. The armies of Nebuchadnezzar marched on Jerusalem, burning the city and dragging its people from their homes. Exiles walked the streets of Babylon, wondering the same questions Lewis, Tolkien, and Dyson discussed on their tree-lined walk in Oxford: what now? The desire to resist burned hot in their hearts, but their arms lacked the strength to set back the clock. Some sought to take up weapons and vent their rage. Others gave up, simply accepted the way things were and blended into Babylon, worshipping its gods and disappearing into its darkness. Others held hope close to their chests and resisted in an unexpected way. God had spoken to his prophet in what was left of Jerusalem and a letter was dispatched to the exiles in Babylon.

> "Thus says the Lord of hosts, the God of Israel, to all the exiles whom I have sent into exile from Jerusalem to Babylon: Build houses and live in them; plant gardens and eat their produce. Take wives and have sons and daughters; take wives for your sons, and give your daughters in marriage, that they may bear sons and daughters; multiply there, and do not decrease. But seek the welfare of the city where I have sent you into exile,

and pray to the Lord on its behalf, for in its welfare you will find your welfare."[3]

The scholar Tim Mackie calls this the way of exile, a way of loyal resistance and protest. It shows a clear path of resistance to the darkness...a way to be a light.[4]

The temptation to fight fire with fire, to define good and evil ourselves is powerful, but it is not what our King asks of us. Yes, "us", not just "them", for though the years have rolled along and the political rule of Nebuchadnezzar has vanished away, the powers he served still hold us in their grip. We are still exiles, wanderers, just as we have been every day since we were removed from beneath the branches of Eden. The intentional decision not to be crushed by the evils of this world, but to be a source of light and beauty is an act of resistance, an act of war against the darkness.

To respond to emptiness with wholeness, to turn even the planning and construction of a home or planting and harvesting a garden into expressions of worship and loyalty is both powerful and accessible. It is not just a possibility for the elite, it is also reachable for you and I. Resistance like this says: we are here, and we intend to stay, we will not be ground down, we will flourish for the Lord is with us. We are not simply in a holding pattern, but are yet active in the fight. Is the church seeking the welfare of the city, or are we simply waiting for the judgment of sinners? Is your town better because your church is there? Does your vision include what lies beyond your walls? Are we "wise as serpents yet gentle as doves[5]"?

The princes of the dark may shed their skin and update their branding, but they remain the same beast. Our calling is not violence or even isolation, but to be oft-visited islands in the cultural rivers of the day. A calling to live side by side with our fellow man, creating joy, praying, being a blessing, and seeking the welfare of

---

3. Jeremiah 29:4–7.
4. BibleProject, "The Way of the Exile."
5. Matthew 10:16.

those around us. A calling to garden, and though the beasts may uproot what we plant, we must continue the dance of Eden.

This is no momentary response to the historical persecution of Old Testament saints, but an ongoing principle which is to define the way God's people live and struggle against the evils around us. The apostle Paul crisscrossed the Empire, planting churches and instructing its people in how to live. The powers of the city of Rome would respond to his message by dragging him beyond the walls of the city and murdering him along the roadway. Before he died, he left a letter to the Christians of that city. Through the blessing of the Holy Spirit, he spoke powerfully to all Christians, teaching us what to do when we face the evils of this world.

> "Do not be overcome by evil, but overcome evil with good."[6]

No revenge killings, no mass exodus from the city, just a call to be what is missing. Purposeful acts of goodness in the face of outright evil. No set list of actions is given, just a direction, for each generation of the church will have to find effective ways of standing in the face of evil. Even when chained in Philippi, the apostle sang in the darkness.

Those who followed this command risked life and limb to protect their Jewish neighbors during the great horror of the Holocaust and earlier strove to bring an end to the slave trade. In ancient Rome, Christians opened their homes to orphans and the abandoned children of the city. All of this was in obedience to be what was missing, worship in motion. Even as you read these words, somewhere a sweet-hearted grandmother is organizing a dinner to feed a family who are burying a loved one. A group of friends is scheduling meals for a mother in labor, and a thoughtful farmer gathers from his garden to share his harvest with his neighbor. At times these acts are great movements worthy of the history books. Others are small acts of intentional joy, leaving an impact only on the faces of people history will never remember. But both are expressions of the Greenway, the Way of the Garden.

---

6. Romans 12:21.

What would it have been like to be a priest enslaved by Babylon? Your whole life was dedicated to service in the temple, only to have the role stripped away, the temple in flames, and your calling left in confusion. The letter from the prophet Jeremiah turned their minds back to an older calling. Once Adam and Eve served in the temple of Eden, loving the Lord their God, tending the trees and the life that walked all around them. Wherever we may tread and no matter what we are forced to leave behind, this calling still remains. Though the temple was taken away, God never left his people. When Adam and Eve were exiled from the garden, they still had access to the God of the garden. Cain and Abel offered sacrifices, and even Cain spoke to the Lord. We will find lives to bless and care for, if not the trees and creatures of Eden, then the families and ground around us. We seek the welfare of the city. We bar the gates against the darkness and walk in the image of the One we serve—the God of gods, the Lord of lords, mighty and awesome.[7]

> "For this is the will of God that by doing good you should put to silence the ignorance of foolish people. Live as people who are free, not using your freedom as a cover-up for evil, but living as servants of God. Honor everyone. Love the brotherhood. Fear God. Honor the emperor."[8]

QUESTIONS FOR REFLECTION

1. In what practical ways can you "seek the welfare of your city" today, even you feel that culture is opposed to your faith?

2. What small, intentional acts of goodness could you practice this week that would serve as resistance to Babylon's values?

3. How can your church balance loyalty to the surrounding community with loyalty to Christ, especially when the two come into conflict?

---

7. Deuteronomy 12:17.
8. 1 Peter 2:15–17.

4. What cultural pressures tempt you to either assimilate into Babylon or fight fire with fire—and how can you instead practice faithful resistance?

5. Adam and Eve's calling was to garden, how can you live out that vocation in your own life?

Chapter 5

The Resistance of a Peaceful People

THE WAYS OF SPEECH in the Bible are not drawn from our modern experience; they reflect ways of life much older and more purposeful than our own. They reflect a people who lived *in* the land not simply *on* it. To them, a well was not an unseen pump somewhere in the basement; it was a central communal hub of life. A place to tell stories, meet friends, and provide for the needs of real life. When Jesus prayed, "Give us this day our daily bread,"[1] his audience wasn't visualizing pre-sliced loaves in plastic bags; it stirred up images of the ovens of the local families, mothers milling flour and baking over hot coals. It meant real life and the thousand common acts performed in your community for your community. It meant provision, care, and fellowship. It meant an ongoing need for God's blessing, and he connected it to an everyday reality, elevating the common act to heavenly spheres.

One phrase the Bible makes use of is a delight to me: "going up to Jerusalem."[2] When I sat in college studying the life of Christ, poring over maps and writing my thoughts into endless notebooks, it bothered me that they used this phrase. To me, going up meant north; my mind was filled with paper maps and satellite

1. Matthew 6:11.
2. Ezra 1:3.

images. I thought how advanced my culture must be compared to theirs because I knew it was foolish to say going "up" to Jerusalem and then walk south, as many people in the Bible did.

I had this foolishness shaken out of me by two events. The first was when I was called to pastor a lovely community of Christians along the banks of the Kanawha River. This wide, mud-colored waterway slowly meandered its way from south to north (unusual for most rivers, but it has a mind of its own). People would chuckle at me if I described a place north of us as "up." If I said something like, "I was running up to Charleston," they would laugh or roll their eyes. To the folks who lived along the Kanawha, up and down were defined by the river, not maps from New York. Up meant upstream and down meant downstream, because the river defined how they thought about their place in the world. They lived in the land not just on it. Its culture had a sense of place that most communities are missing, not just another carbon copy of a wider world, but an Appalachian people marked by the river which had given life to their towns.

The second event which opened the doors of this Biblical phrase to my mind was actually going up to Jerusalem. Everywhere seemed to be up; it is a land of hills and valleys and Jerusalem is not simply on *a* mountain it is on *the* mountain. Just as the river had oriented the lives of my friends, Jerusalem oriented the people of Scripture. It was the center regardless of what the maps say. It was not attempting to make a geographical point, it was speaking about the world as they lived it.

Standing on the ancient cracked stones south of the Temple Mount, I examined a wide staircase which once ascended from the old City of David to the heights of the Temple Mount. I was struck by the skill apparent in what these ancient artists had left behind, but could not understand a feature which I thought at the time was a flaw in the construction. None of the steps were uniform in size or depth. One step would require you to lift your foot high to step up, others did not; some were wide, others narrow. I thought to myself, "They must not have known how important uniformity is in stairs; you could trip and fall." I doubt OSHA would have approved. I was surprised to learn that what I thought of as an imperfection was really a purposeful decision, an architect's attempt to create a sense of slow purposeful worship. My tour guide informed me that to ascend the stairs, you needed to bow your head, watch where you stepped, slow down, and cease to hurry. Those construction workers accomplished a deed of such long-lasting devotion that it staggers my mind. Instead of seeking uniformity and mere function, they built worship into the stairs. An act of such creative functionality that my own efforts appear dim in the light of their creativity. A work of art intended to be trod underfoot as it lifts you into the temple's court. To their mind, ease and convenience were second to beauty and reverence. My pride and chronological snobbery had blinded me to a reality that had been praising God for thousands of years. What other wonders has my arrogance caused me to overlook?

Of course, there are Christian traditions who make great use of art, but I notice that it is almost always accompanied by an elitist attitude. Look but don't touch, or this is only for the clergy; the table is seldom spread for all. It reminds me more of a china cabinet filled with beautiful dishes intended for the important people than it does those humble stairs. Don't mistake me; if nothing is set aside as special, we will not see it as wonderful. But I think we are missing something. It is easy to venerate an icon or a piece of art behind the velvet ropes of a museum, but I believe that God looks on the lowly acts of worship with the same joy as the great.

Once, when speaking to the crowds who had gathered to hear Christ speak, He said: "And whoever gives one of these little ones even a cup of cold water because he is a disciple, truly, I say to you, he will by no means lose his reward."[3]

No call for cathedrals to be built in his name, no miracle shaking the doubts of the lost. Jesus intentionally uses a lowly act of generosity, an act that would have been at home in Eden. Not just sharing water because some one needs it, not just doing something nice or because its what we want others to do for us, but to act as a representative of the Kingdom of God. I will give

---

3. Matthew 10:42.

it to you because I am a disciple of Christ, or I will give to them because they are servants of Christ. No blowing your own horn, no bait and switch sermon, just an act of generous worship between you and God which blesses another. There must always be times of personal devotion and worship, and there will naturally be moments of sacrificial giving, but there must also be moments when we act for the joy of it, for the beauty it brings into the world. It is an expression of God's grace, a time when we act like our Father who created not out of need but out of love and when our cup runneth over.[4]

When medieval monks recorded the words of Scripture, they hung art around the words like fruit hanging from a tree. When masons constructed new churches, their love and art moved the stone like water, leaving stories and beauty etched in its floors and walls. The beautiful, many-hewed windows of our grandfather's churches still proclaim the gospel even after the pulpits have fallen silent. Whittling woodworkers turned stumps into crosses, families decorated the posts of their houses with beautiful designs, and town squares were filled with music. Christmas trees were covered with lights and memories. This beautiful artistry is an expression of the Greenway—the Way of Eden.

Years ago when visiting Galilee, I went to the Church of the Beatitudes, built on a site where Christians have gathered since the fourth century to reflect on our Lord's Sermon on the Mount. Hustling along like ducklings following our guide, we bee-lined for the church. I don't remember if I ever made it inside the building, for I was stopped in my tracks long before we reached its doors. There, with the sea behind them, great palm trees swayed in the wind, olive trees rustled their tiny leaves, and the bush-lined paths and plots of flowers all called my heart to worship. The church itself is lovely, but it was the garden that sang the glory of God. The smell of flowers hung in the air along with the sound of laughing children as fellow tourists drank in the sight. All of it was prepared to greet you like a well-cooked meal laid out upon the table for the guests to enjoy. The garden was no mere decoration or

4. Psalm 23:5.

landscaping, but a choir calling all around to worship. I had never experienced its like. The gardeners who tended its branches had, in my opinion, achieved something no church auditorium ever had. We need more of that.

We need churches, communities of Christ-followers who want to be more, more than a concert and a pep talk. Communities who explore the Scriptures with the same excitement as ocean divers on a reef, hearing afar the great doctrines of the faith calling to them like whales singing in the deep. People who not only love the text but have been changed by it, who wield what power they have to create little pockets of Eden. To love the Lord their God with all their hearts, all their souls, and all their mind.[5]

We must not expect our efforts to look the same, for culture, interest, style, and generation will all change the approach we take. Creativity is not only permissible it is required. When gardeners set out to prune, they know that all trees grow in unique twists and turns; there is no correct number of branches or leaves, but there is a common set of principles which guide their hands. We also are gardeners. We may not tend the trees of Eden, but we are to be a force for good, for joy, for holiness. The principles which guide us are not ours to set, but are revealed in Scripture. Let us "do justly, love mercy, and walk humbly before the Lord our God."[6] The principalities and powers whisper of another way, but when God's people resist the darkness, it will look like going up to Jerusalem.

QUESTIONS FOR REFLECTION

1. How can you bring beauty and creativity into ordinary life as an act of worship?
2. What simple, everyday acts (like a "cup of cold water") could you practice this week as resistance to Babylon and witness to Christ?

---

5. Deuteronomy 6:4.
6. Micah 6:8.

3. In what ways might your church incorporate beauty, and creativity, into its life together to reflect God's glory?
4. How can you cultivate a mindset of living "in the land, not just on it"—in your community?
5. What is the significance of the uneven temple steps, and what does their design teach us about worship and legacy?

Chapter 6

Dominion or Dominance?

THERE WERE OFTEN BEARS in my grandparents' yard. They stumbled down the mountain in search of trash cans and fruit trees, and each grandchild was well aware of how to handle the situation should one of these mountain wanderers find their way into the yard. You get big, arms in the air, feet spread apart, make a lot of noise, and then get to the house. We shouted "Hey Mr. Bear," or made ridiculous noises trying to let the bear know that they weren't alone and should go away. In my experience, bears are oblivious, single-minded creatures. Once they smell an apple tree, they notice very little except the apples. They are curious, awkward creatures, and the ones around their house always looked offended and confused that we were there. The closest I ever got to a bear was when I spent the night at my grandparents' home as a young child. My granny woke me up when she heard the bears plundering her apple tree in the backyard. Holding my hand, she quietly walked me to the screen door and turned on the porch light. Like a bolt of lightning, sudden brightness flooded the steps, revealing the face and portly body of a very confused black bear, inches from the screen door. I am quite certain it nearly had a heart attack. The bear made a valiant attempt to get all its limbs under control, then stumbled and trotted its way back to the mountain. In typical West

Virginian fashion, it is a wild and wonderful place. The mountains are places of joy and adventure, but they are also untamed and dangerous, and though care was needed to navigate them, we didn't avoid them; we loved them.

As our world spun into a new millennium, epic rains fell on the mountains behind my grandparents' home. Depending on who you ask, you may hear tales about the strip-mining companies, scraping the mountain tops away as they hunted for more coal, but regardless of what caused it, the rains and the rocks, the mud and the sludge washed that house away. All that remains of those memories now are the flowers my grandparents planted around the house. Like candles at a vigil, they remember where the walls once stood. A rectangle of green and the jewel-hewn blossoms refused to be moved even when the house's foundation shifted and the walls were broken down. I have returned to that hallowed piece of earth many times, and I am always moved by the testament of those living expressions of love and home. My grandparents have long since gone home to the Lord, but the works of their hands still testify of a place of safety and joy, a place where the love of God was taught and lived.

Long ago when God created Adam and Eve, he gave them responsibilities which made them unique among the physical creations of this world. They were created to image Him, to subdue the earth, and to have dominion over it.[1] Here we find a difference of values and meaning. Do the words *subdue* and *dominion* mean the same thing to Babylon as to the Kingdom of God? Most assuredly they do not. Yet when the Christian hears these commands, we are more likely to hear it with the rhythm of Babylon ringing in our hearts. We hear the serpent's twisted voice—"Did God actually say?" He urges a different interpretation, a different motive, and a different goal. Can't we read these words to mean we can do as we please? Can we be excused for treating the earth and its creatures as our own private property, to be used and abused as we see fit?

Historically, people have interpreted subduing the earth and having dominion over its creatures as license to do as we please, but

---

1. Genesis 1:26–31.

power in the Kingdom of Heaven is wielded differently than this world expects. We cannot have dominion if we will not image our Lord; the darkness of Babylon will whisper to you, urging you to seek dominance over creation, to manipulate it for your own glory. Motives matter and they direct our actions; the following account will show that we aren't the first to look at things upside down.

Matthew chapter twenty reveals a moment from the life of Jesus where at least two of his disciples were planning ahead for the Kingdom. In a display worthy of the court drama of any ancient king, the family of Zebedee executes a plan to secure power in Christ's kingdom. As Jesus is leading his disciples to Jerusalem, preparing them for his crucifixion, the mother of James and John, skirts flowing around her, approaches the Lord, kneels down in the dirt, and asks that her sons be given the highest positions in Christ's Kingdom. The scene would have fit right into any monarch's court; a bit of manipulation, a bit of showmanship. Who knows, it could work. Instead, it ignited an argument filled with anger and hurt feelings. Jesus used the moment to draw attention to the twisted nature of Babylon and how humanity views power by contrasting how God expects those with dominion to behave.

> ". . . You know that the rulers of the Gentiles lord it over them, and their great ones exercise authority over them. It shall not be so among you. But whoever would be great among you must be your servant, and whoever would be first among you must be your slave, even as the Son of Man came not to be served but to serve, and to give his life as a ransom for many."[2]

I do not think when God endowed Adam and Eve with dominion he was empowering tyrants but was instead equipping servants. He created us in his image and the Son of Man came to seek and to save that which was lost.[3]

Was there ever a man greater than Jesus? Of course not. He is the King of Kings, the Lord of lords, and when he walked the dusty paths of this world in human form, he showed us what mankind

2. Matthew 20:25b-28.
3. Luke 19:10.

was meant to be. Not pride-filled princes who bend the earth to their will but humble, lowly, not seeking to be served but to serve. At times we look more like leeches than shepherds, vampires rather than gardeners. For shame, how can we image God when we wrap ourselves in the ways of Babylon? Someone out there is rolling their eyes and calling me a tree hugger or guessing at my political affiliation, but I am simply asking if, when life's trials end and we face our Maker, will He say, "Well done, good and faithful servant?"[4] Is the self-obsession we treasure and the comfort we crave a worthy substitute for loving what God has made and caring for it? I do not mean caring for the earth because it is nice or good for the environment, but because by caring for it we image God. When we care for the places we are, it shows the loving nature of the Lord, it brings Him glory, it becomes worship.

The city planner designing a playground, the young couple buying plants, the elderly gardener watering the flowers, the painter with their brushes, the parent packing lunches, the musician writing furiously, the barista in the shop all stand on the edge of worship, and if only they will do so to the glory of God, they will testify of the creator and keeper of all things. These common acts can become small but lovely lights in the twilight, acts of resistance to a world gone mad, intentional attempts to subdue the darkness, expressions of dominion. We need not be swept along with the evils and hollow promises of this world. Nature may be red in tooth and claw,[5] but like Daniel in the lions' den, we may confound the fiery darts of the wicked one. We may have been swept away from the rivers of Eden, but let us swim upstream, not down.

Dominion is not a matter of riches or being obeyed; it is a calling, a responsibility to image God, treating the world and people around me as Christ would. We are not seeking to dominate others, but to exercise dominion. The gardener cannot force the plant to grow, but they can encourage it, they can struggle to create conditions where the plant can thrive. The seeds may never sprout, the tree may not produce fruit, but the gardener longs to see it

4. Matthew 5:23.
5. Tennyson, *In Memoriam A.H.H.*, 59.

happen. We do not control the ends, but we can faithfully work and keep the garden.

> "What then is Apollos? What is Paul? Servants through whom you believed, as the Lord assigned to each. I planted, Apollos watered, but God gave the growth. So neither he who plants nor he who waters is anything, but only God who gives the growth. He who plants and he who waters are one, and each will receive his wages according to his labor. For we are God's fellow workers. You are God's field, God's building."[6]

Our Lord has placed us in a wonderful world full of mystery and beauty. I pray that his people will remember that the world in which we live is more than just kindling to be burned in our quest for wealth and convenience; it is a treasure entrusted into our hands. Let the people of God rejoice in what He has made,[7] and in our care for the land in which we live, let us show the love of God. Let us wield dominion and leave the places we dwell safer, better and more beautiful. Let us garden; let us worship.

QUESTIONS FOR REFLECTION

1. How can you practice "dominion" in your daily responsibilities without slipping into dominance or self-centeredness or bossiness?
2. What practical steps can you take to reflect Christ's servant-leadership in the way you use influence or authority?
3. How can ordinary acts—gardening, creating, planning, teaching, serving—become worshipful expressions of dominion?
4. In what ways might you need to resist cultural voices that equate power with dominance, wealth, or control?
5. How can your church model godly dominion in its stewardship of people, resources, and creation?

---

6. 1 Corinthians 3:5-9.
7. Psalm 118:24.

Chapter 7

Songs of Exile

PERCHED ATOP THE PALATINE Hill, along the looping banks of the River Tiber, the people of a small village scratched wealth from the fertile fields surrounding them and from the trade that flowed by their hilltop den. Slowly, by hook or by crook, they spread the net of dominance over their neighbors, forcing them to kneel in submission to their weapons and will. The eagle standards of their armies marched in all directions until the Mediterranean became a Roman lake. The land of Israel, no longer independent, became a satellite of the hills of Rome. The tread of Roman boots and the heavy hand of its tax collectors sowed seeds of bitterness and helplessness in the hearts of the common people.

By the time our Lord walked the land, the Pharisees and Sadducees no longer saw Rome as a foe, but as a tool to be used to wield more power. Indeed, one of their reasons for murdering Jesus was their fear that his acts of beauty, kindness, and truth, that the Way of Eden which he embodied would upset their power, their dominance. Better he be murdered than that they should change.[1] They had no knowledge that God would use their violent natures to unleash salvation for humanity, for God is able to bring beauty even out of our own bent hearts. They simply wanted to control the

---

1. John 11:48–50.

situation, and their default method was hate. Jesus modeled a different way, a way given to us in the greenness of Eden. Dominion does involve resistance, but not as Babylon teaches. Instead, it is a way of resistance which he makes clear in his Sermon on the Mount.

> "Blessed are the merciful, for they shall obtain mercy. Blessed are the pure in heart, for they shall see God. Blessed are the peacemakers, for they shall be called sons of God. Blessed are those who are persecuted for righteousness' sake, for theirs is the kingdom of heaven."[2]

We respond with mercy because we have been wronged. We strive to let no shadow of Babylon grow in our hearts. We seek not only to be peaceful but to make peace, doing so in the full knowledge that these are acts of resistance and the enemy will meet them with force. It may seem simplistic or naive, but what do we do? How do we put feet to our faith? If violence is not the way, and hatred is forbidden, what can we do? The voice of Jesus will guide us if we have ears that will listen. He chose several injustices common in his generation and showed how to overcome them by wielding the ways of the Kingdom of God against the powers of this world.

A Roman soldier had the right to force any resident of Israel to act as his servant, as a pack animal carrying his baggage for one mile. Jesus did not encourage his followers to kill the soldier or to run away. Instead, he puts forward a strange and unusual counterpoint.

> "And if anyone forces you to go one mile, go with him two miles."[3]

Far from being a simple good deed, it is the refusal to be broken by the iron hand of the Dark. You may steal a mile of my life, but I can resist your violence by freely gifting you another. I am not broken by your abuse; I am stronger than you think. Unjust laws will not take from us the dominion God has entrusted to us; you have not taken control because we are yet free. It is mercy

---

2. Matthew 5:7–10.
3. Matthew 5:41.

in motion, literally bearing another's burden, not because they've earned it, but because they haven't. It is an act of loving resistance. The Darkness will twist and change its attacks. Creativity and flexibility amongst God's people will be needed for the fight, but the words of Christ guide us into this battle; they direct our resistance. The works of the darkness must be met with the fruits of the Spirit.

The Faithful of the Lord can not expect to walk this battlefield untouched by the violence of Babylon; indeed, the crown of the martyr will always loom before God's people. Babylon will seek to shame you, to break your spirit. Our Lord knew this. He does not call us into mere conflict avoidance; instead Christ shows his people how to wield peace against hate. If an enemy strikes you across the face, turn the other cheek.[4] Violence is met with peace, shame is met with honor when we absorb the blow and invite another. We will not lie down in the face of violence, we show that the foe has failed to break us; we are still on our feet, and we refuse to become like you. It is neither a passive reaction nor is it cowardliness, but an intentional act of resistance against the Darkness. To bear this burden is an expression of strength and loyalty to Christ who also turned his cheek to his oppressors, bore the cross, and made blindingly obvious the Kingdom of God.

Babylon will seek to force you into its mold, to impose its values and image onto you; we may not be able to respond with world-shaking power, but the act of turning the other cheek is available to all of us. Jesus didn't focus on the great as much as he did the poor, the average people of his day. Should the moment occur when my actions can be global in their impact, I hope I rise to the occasion, but that situation seems unlikely; that does not mean, however, my efforts are pointless or powerless. It just means that my battlefield is more local and that my mission field is where my feet are. I can't change the whole world, but I can be a faithful witness wherever I stand, choosing to resist the ugliness of sin and seeking to be like my Father.

The faithful, small actions of loyal imagers of God are powerful not only in isolation but in their collective impact. A castle may

---

4. Matthew 5:39.

be built of massive stones, but most are collections of thousands of small, shaped rocks purposefully placed and locked together. Do we intentionally shape the stones, the actions of our lives, or do we simply react out of the impulses and shadows of our own bent hearts? Do we view our efforts through the glasses of individualism or do we seek to work together, encouraging our communities, laying aside personal ambition for the service of one another? Honoring our King, we each esteem others as better than ourselves.[5]

We too often think of the walls of the church as a means of keeping the world out and not a place of beauty and instruction, preparing the people of Christ to storm the strongholds of Babylon. A place where the church gathers and is lifted up in worship and communion. Does the church support and equip her congregation to wage war, or do we simply put on a good show and collect an offering? I fear we invest in the flashy and yawn at the faithful. I suppose what I'm trying to say is that though we speak with the tongues of men and angels and have not love, we have become as a sounding brass or a clanging cymbal.[6]

Is that the sound of Christ's people today? What does the world around us hear? Have we abandoned the ringing of trumpets for the clanging of cymbals? Has YouTube replaced evensong? Has grumbling uprooted praise? A pastor on TV is more likely to be seen as a con-artist than as a shepherd. Would we see our enemies broken rather than forgiven? My friend, the darkness has covered our communities so thoroughly that even small sparks of light will be seen.

One of the most powerful sermons I ever heard was not preached from a pulpit. It was a married couple at the church I attended in college who opened their home to students after the service. They fed us, let us wash our laundry and watch football. Living in a dorm where laundry meant quarters and television was not allowed, to know we were wanted in their home was a slice of heaven. She would ask us questions about the sermon or what we

5. Philippians 2:2–5.
6. I Corinthians 13:1.

were reading while we drank coffee at the dinner table, and her quiet husband would often ask us to help him split wood for the stove that heated the living room. While he split and we stacked the wood, he would talk about his faith and dispense mountain wisdom. In short, they walked the Greenway. I saw Eden in their love and heard Christ in their voices.

Church is not a place to attend, it is a thing to be. Let us be people of steady lights in the darkness, filled with Spirit-led acts of love and the song of an exile longing for Eden.

QUESTIONS FOR REFLECTION

1. What events in your daily life could become "second-mile" moments of mercy, generosity, or patience?
2. In what ways do the Beatitudes (Matt. 5:7–10) redefine what resistance looks like in the Kingdom of God?
3. In what practical ways can your church equip believers to resist Babylon through discipleship, hospitality, and service rather than entertainment?
4. What small acts of light could you create in your own community?
5. How can you and your community ensure that the "sound" the world hears from the church is love, joy, and worship rather than grumbling or cynicism?

Chapter 8

The Garden of Sorrow

NOT ALL GARDENS ARE sunshine and flowers; some are made of shadow and stone and lie deep in the forest, their sleepy broad leaves and deep greens praising the God of the Garden still. Subtle and abstract, bereft of fruit and bright color, they are nonetheless beautiful. Our lives are not a progression of cheer and happiness; this world will simply not allow it. Here, where we experience sorrow and grief, we find that fear and loss grow with effortless ease. The abomination of racism, the heartbreak of shattered love, greed, abuse, and a regiment of evils too numerous to list leave the Christian heart hurting and weeping. Yet even in sorrow, we can find beauty; even in the midst of pain, we can resist Babylon.

Once when the judges ruled ancient Israel, hunger drove the family of Elimelech from Bethlehem into exile. As is so often the case, their attempt to escape tragedy proved to be just the beginning of heartbreak. Though at first the danger seemed to have passed, tragedy followed them and struck Elimelech down, leaving a grieving family striving to find a new life in a strange land. His sons both married, but before they could reap the joys of their new life, they followed their father into early graves.[1]

---

1. Ruth 1:1–5.

Sorrow on sorrow left Elimelech's wife, Naomi, and her two daughters-in-law alone, afraid, and draped in the cloak of grief. With little choice but to return home in poverty, Naomi set her eyes towards Bethlehem. A moment filled with tears and broken dreams has left us with one of the most beautiful acts of resistance against sorrow in all Scripture. Naomi attempted to send her daughters away and to walk in loneliness and grief back to the home she had been forced to abandon, but Ruth, refusing to be broken or to allow Naomi to face the dangers of life alone, spoke up with one of the clearest examples of the Greenway that I have ever seen.

> "But Ruth said, 'Do not urge me to leave you or to return from following you. For where you go I will go, and where you lodge I will lodge. Your people shall be my people, and your God my God. Where you die I will die, and there will I be buried. May the Lord do so to me and more also if anything but death parts me from you.'"[2]

She doesn't just think happy thoughts or distract herself from evil with the pleasures of the day, she marches against her grief, declaring loyalty, faithfulness, and friendship. Ruth is not broken by the experience, nor does she simply survive it. She fights it. This is no passive, inward-focused soul. She began to garden even in the rains of grief.

When depression grips my heart tight and my mind fills with darkness, God calls me to struggle against it, and he helps me to do so. I may not appear to make great strides; indeed, sometimes even the act of remaining on my feet is the result of an almighty struggle. The world may not see it as much of an accomplishment, but my resistance is not a gift for them but to my Father. It is an act of worship.

We would all have forgiven Ruth if the sorrow had broken her, but it did not, and her proclamation is a light of hope to me when my depression will not leave me be. She not only longs for a friend who will stand by her, she longs to be a friend who will

---

2. Ruth 1:16–17.

The Garden of Sorrow

stand against the storms of life. In a moment when she must have felt empty and purposeless, she reaches into the ash and makes something. She creates family. I can not help but see the hidden hand of God in her life, and in her struggle I hear the anguished cries of Adam and Eve as they were driven from the garden; yet still they taught their children to offer sacrifices before the Lord. I long for this in my own life.

Not the ignoring of sorrow but the conquest of it. Like a flower defiantly growing in the cracks of a sidewalk, it displays the power of life and the goodness of God. The pain is sharp, the disappointment is crushing, and in those moments, we must ask ourselves what we will do. Will we lie down and let the darkness overcome us or summon what strength we have and resist? Pop culture Christianity has little space for those who mourn, seeing it somehow as a departure from God's plan for us, but Jesus did not seem to think that those who are bearing the weight of sorrow were failing; indeed, he calls them blessed.[3] The sorrowful can image God in ways the laughing cannot. Comfort will come, but while we stand in the shadow of grief, while we yet mourn, we image God.

Christ wept beside Lazarus' tomb, the psalmist hung his harp in the willows by the waters of Babylon, refusing to sing for his captors, and when all creation lay defiled by the twisted hearts of mankind and the bloody hands of the fallen sons of God, Scripture tells us that the sight of it grieved God to his heart.[4] Is there not an entire book of the Bible called Lamentations? The sticky sweet voice of pop culture Christianity may have no room for those who mourn, but God still sees them. He understands, even if those who sit in the sunshine do not, that lamentation can also be worship. The prophets left behind them words of both joy and sorrow, but the Spirit of God moved Jeremiah, the weeping prophet, to write not one but two books. Giving voice to his sorrow, he poured words into the page, like wine poured onto the altar, a drink offering of sorrow.

3. Matthew 5:4.
4. Genesis 6:6.

"Oh that my head were waters, and my eyes a fountain of tears, that I might weep day and night for the slain of the daughter of my people!"[5]

The apostle Paul echoes this emotion in the book of Romans:

"I have great sorrow and unceasing anguish in my heart."[6]

Can we be forgiving if there is nothing to forgive? Can we be long suffering if we are not suffering? Need we pray that God would 'put a guard on my mouth'[7] if we are not tempted to lash out? Sorrow is part of our story. We cannot choose what weapon the enemy will strike us with, but God is with us, and in his presence, we can refuse to let it break us. There is room for deep color as well as bright in Eden. Let us rejoice with those that rejoice and weep with those that weep,[8] and as we do so, we remember the joy of the resurrection is only possible because of the sorrow of the cross.

QUESTIONS FOR REFLECTION

1. How does Ruth's vow to Naomi (Ruth 1:16–17) serve as an act of resistance against grief and despair?
2. Why does the chapter describe lamentation—like Jeremiah's and Paul's—as worship rather than weakness?
3. In what way does Jesus' beatitude "Blessed are those who mourn" (Matt. 5:4) challenge pop culture Christianity's view of sorrow?
4. How can your church create space for lament—valuing the voices of the sorrowful rather than silencing them?
5. What does the metaphor of flowers growing in cracks or gardens of shadow teach us about beauty in seasons of suffering?

5. Jeremiah 9:1.
6. Romans 9:2.
7. Psalm 141:3.
8. Romans 12:15.

Chapter 9

Trees Planted by Streams of Water

ON THE SLOPES OF a hillside in California grows the oldest tree in all the world. Due to his old age and cantankerous nature, his location remains undisclosed, but this bristlecone pine named Methuselah was already over two thousand years old when Jesus walked the earth. He sprouted on the mountain side around the same time the first ditches of Stonehenge were being dug. My mind short circuits just thinking about it.

Having been raised in the forests of Appalachia, there are few things as beautiful to me as trees. Stately magnolias, colorful dogwoods, scrappy pines; they are all pictures of strength, fortitude, and life. I assume because I grew up surrounded by them, it has never been a surprise to me that God talks about people like trees. We seem to have been designed to be companions. We breathe in their oxygen, and they breathe in our carbon dioxide. We long for the shade and fruit of their branches, and their presence has always seemed to make things better.

The Bible has intricately linked the language of trees and mankind together. We are to be fruitful,[1] we are to be rooted and

---

1. Genesis 1:28.

built up.[2] The judgment of sinners is described as being cut off.[3] Children are called seed,[4] rebellious kings are "cut down,"[5] and even wisdom is described as a Tree of Life.[6] Our rebellion began under the branches of trees. Our salvation was made possible by the Tree of Calvary, and the Bible ends by describing the throne of God and the trees that stand before his throne.

In modern English, we make a distinction between a tree and wood. Deep down in the way we see the world, trees are products to be used and not creatures to be cared for. Biblical Hebrew doesn't make this distinction; the word for a living tree and what the tree is made of are the same word: ʿēṣ. Vines are trees in the text, so are staffs; the cross, even Noah's ark, is a collection of trees bound together to save the animals and their caretakers. Aaron's flowering staff[7] is a living tree, not drawing life from roots in the ground but from the will of the Father. God provides clear water for Israel by instructing Moses to cast an ʿēṣ into a bitter pool.[8] In the book of Esther, the word ʿēṣ describes the gallows on which Haman met his end.[9] David carries a staff and a sling to face the giant Goliath;[10] Joseph is described as a fruitful branch;[11] even the Messiah is described as both a branch[12] and a shoot from the stump of Jesse.[13] All these are not simply bits of wood; they are trees.

It may seem strange to the modern reader how often the Bible, a book famous for a lack of details and scene setting, mentions trees. We must remember that the Bible is an ancient book

2. Colossians 2:7.
3. Psalm 34:15–16.
4. Genesis 22:17–18.
5. Isaiah 10:33 & Daniel 4:23–25.
6. Proverbs 3:18.
7. Numbers 17:8.
8. Exodus 15:24.
9. Esther 7:9.
10. 1 Samuel 17:40.
11. Genesis 49:22.
12. Jeremiah 23:5.
13. Isaiah 11:1.

and uses an ancient world and its tools to reveal heavenly truths. When the Bible moves to poetry and gifts to us the ancient songs that we call the Psalms, its very first bit of music is a calling for us to be like a tree. It is the cry of the people of the garden longing for fellowship with God and to be as He made us to be. To have roots, a place, and a purpose.

Trees are not only symbols of wealth and comfort; they are a force of life on the earth. They give joy, shelter, and comfort to those around them. Is there a better picture of what the followers of Christ should be like? Resisting the forces of death and decay, we reach for the heavens, brightening the lives of those around us. We bear the fruit of the Spirit and are filled with unseen power. The Kingdom of God is like this: it is a seed buried in the soil, dead to the eye of the observer, but in it, unseen yet very real, is the power of life. Even the smallest seeds can grow into complex and wonderful treasures of the garden, and so can we.

By a stream in Virginia grows a sycamore tree. I have no intention of telling you where it grows, for by its side flows a stream filled with trout, and no fisherman worth his salt willingly reveals such a place. When depression held me tight and I was broken in heart, it was there, asking nothing, simply sheltering me from the sun as I sought peace. When I was filled with joy at the birth of my son, its silent presence gave me a place to gather my thoughts as I wrapped my mind around the responsibilities of fatherhood. When I was simply seeking the fun of chasing trout or testing an amateurish fly I had tied in the garage, it was there, waiting for my return. It asks for nothing, drawing its strength from the stream and earth, and pouring out blessings and rest.

Was there ever a time when the world so needed Christ's church to be like a tree? In an age of noise and self-indulgence, trees are almost a rebuke to our obsessions. Yet when the troubles of our loud lives leave us empty and overwhelmed, a walk among the trees provides respite that the culture never can. They pull us into a different, more permanent world, and they draw our minds towards heaven.

Can we still make spaces of rest and art? Can we still create a home for poetry and contemplation? Do such things still have a place in a modern church? Our church buildings are hardly examples of maximized potential, and our emphasis seems to be focused only on a stage. Is there no room for moving beyond the Sunday service, for emphasizing being like a tree? Our culture has many tools for private study, and we have mastered isolation, but many long for community; it's not something we can schedule, for life is messy and busy, but as a forest is a permanent space for wandering and being, we surely can try.

One of the things that struck me hard during a recent trip to Jerusalem was the Western Wall of the Temple Mount. I knew it to be a place of prayer, and sometimes tears, but it is also a place of community, of study, celebration, and composition. It has its own library, chairs and tables filled with friends reading the Scriptures in the shadow of history. I watched young men with pens in their hands and poetry in their hearts worship the Lord through the art of writing. I heard the voices of women singing prayers together, and watched as rabbis answered questions for those who were confused. I saw artists with their sketchbooks, and even families dancing in celebration. It wasn't a scheduled event, but a culture intentionally being like trees.

My heart aches at the memory, for my own culture places little value on such things. We expect individuals to pursue such things on their own time. I long to hear of churches intentionally encouraging acts of worship beyond the Sunday service: of prayer gardens planted and cared for, of churches investing in equipment for writers, podcasters, and artists. Can we no longer create beautiful spaces designed for writing or reading? Can we not move beyond just appreciating creativity and instead seek to cultivate it? To garden, to tend and keep those growing around us. Perhaps these ideas are too old-fashioned, but I miss them; I do not want to simply hand them over to the secular world. We can do better; we can garden.

QUESTIONS FOR REFLECTION

1. What practices can help you live like a tree—rooted in God, fruitful, and providing rest for others?
2. How could your church cultivate spaces (gardens, art, music, study, community) that reflect the life of the Spirit rather than just programs?
3. What "streams" (Scripture, worship, fellowship, prayer) have been meaningful in your own life?
4. Who in your life needs the "shade" of your presence and how can you provide it this week?
5. How might creating beauty (art, writing, music, hospitality) serve as a form of worship and resistance to Babylon's emptiness?

Chapter 10

Music in the Trees

COME MY FRIEND, LEAVE behind the burden of the day and sit with me for awhile. The sun has sunk behind the mountains, and darkness blankets the forests of Appalachia. Twilight in the mountains is good for your soul. The heat of sun slowly fades from the air, and the sounds of the forest shift and change.

To sit with friends, in the cool of a summer night, watching the stars slowly slip into place as they step on the stage of the night sky is one of life's greatest pleasures. It has its own music. The barred owl's call replaces the chattering of song birds while the rumble of coal trucks cease, giving way to one of the most enchanting sounds of the forest. High up in trees, between us and the stars, a choir awakens. Spring peepers begin calling to one another through the branches of the forest. Not isolated bursts of noise but what seems to be hundreds of tiny voices singing in the shadows.

Perhaps you aren't familiar with spring peepers. They are tree frogs bearing the mark of the cross of St. Andrew on their backs. They don't croak like their mud-wallowing brethren, but with high-pitched clear voices they "peep" to one another, sounding more like sleigh-bells hung from a horse's bridle rather than the croaking bull frogs of the marshes. Creatures smaller than your smallest finger, all singing the same song, they are unmistakable

Music in the Trees

and unforgettable, an earthly voice echoing the seraphim who cry "Holy, Holy, Holy" in the temple of the Lord.

To be sure, the dangers of the hills are still there. The call of coyotes is hard to miss, or the ponderous tread of bears stomping through the leaves, popping their jaws as they wander hungrily in the gloom. Even the occasional scream of a mountain lion is not unheard of, but these are not the voice that shapes the night. Danger may yet walk in the woods, but these tiny frogs are the sound of summer nights, faithfully perched high in the trees as they sing.

I tell you this not to praise the land of my youth but to ask the church: can you not see our calling in the trees? Babylon may walk the darkness of our world, its claws and teeth yet sharp, its lies and hatred unmistakable, but just as those frogs fill the wind with music, so can the church. Not because we are big and powerful, but because we have climbed high and will not be silenced. Because a thousand small acts of worship can not be mistaken for anything but the Kingdom of God. If we could stop shouting about what offends us, stop walking about with a scowl and an up-turned nose, perhaps we might be seen as the oaks of righteousness, the planting of the Lord, that he may be glorified.[1]

We are called not only to refuse the grip of sin, but to work and keep the garden. Not simply to refrain but to create. If Adam and Eve had ignored the beauty and joy of the garden to only focus on the danger of the forbidden tree, they would not have imaged the God who called them to have dominion. Our faith must not be defined by what we reject but by what we embrace.

In the generation before our Lord was born, the famous Rabbi Hillel taught this concept to his disciples: what is hateful to you, do not do to your neighbor. Excellent advice, one which would leave the world better and brighter, but when Christ spoke to us he changed the voice and direction of this truth. He urged his people not simply to cease from doing evil but to do good.

---

1. Isaiah 61:3.

"So whatever you wish that others would do to you, do also to them."[2]

He changed it from passive to active, moving its focus from self to community. Personal holiness is vital; however, it is not the end of our calling, but a beginning. If my cup overflows, let me fill other's cups as well. Neither saying is evil, but one of them is richer, fuller, and more beautiful. One is lack and one is substance.

Christ once rebuked the Pharisees and scribes of Israel, and in his words I hear a warning for myself as well. They focused on what they could not do, eaten up by legalism and single-minded in the avoidance of the appearance of worldliness. They appeared holy, but were filled with the fruits of Death.

> "For you are like whitewashed tombs, which outwardly appear beautiful, but within are full of dead people's bones and all uncleanness. So you also outwardly appear righteous to others, but within you are full of hypocrisy and lawlessness."[3]

I do not want to be a grave stone, I want to be like those mountain frogs who make beauty out of silence. If the heavens declare the glory of God,[4] why should I be content with an inward pointing heart? I not only long to tell you what God can do for you, I want to join Him in being a blessing to others.

The real power of spring peepers is not in the beauty of the individual, but in their collective voice. That is what moves my heart. Long before humanity walked those mountains, the music of the peepers called out, faithful even without an audience. They do not sing for us, but for something unseen. These mountains have always called to me. Draped in mist and mystery, they have stood by me even when my heart was overwhelmed in sorrow. In their shadows I have glimpsed Calvary, and in their song I have heard the echoes of heaven. They are not just scenery, for no photograph of them can come close to the experience of walking alone

2. Matthew 7:12.
3. Matthew 23:27–28.
4. Psalm 19:1.

in their forests. They are a place to be, and in them my mind has seen truths of the Kingdom of God. My friend, let us cast aside the voices of Babylon, and climb the slopes; let us press on that we may hear the voice of God whisper to us:

> "Well done, good and faithful servant. You have been faithful over a little; I will set you over much. Enter into the joy of your master."[5]

QUESTIONS FOR REFLECTION

1. What "songs of worship"—small acts of goodness, beauty, or kindness—can you add to the chorus of the church this week?

2. How does Jesus' reworking of Rabbi Hillel's teaching (Matt. 7:12) shift holiness from passive avoidance of evil to active creation of good?

3. In what ways can your community embody Isaiah's vision of being "oaks of righteousness"—steady, rooted, and fruitful?

4. How can your church cultivate collective acts of blessing that echo louder than individual efforts?

5. How do the spring peepers function as a metaphor for the church's calling in a dark and dangerous world?

---

5. Matthew 25:21.

Bibliography

Augustine. *Confessions*. Translated by Henry Chadwick. Oxford World's Classics. Oxford: Oxford University Press, 1991.
BibleProject. "The Way of the Exile." Accessed October 3, 2025. Video, 5:20. https://bibleproject.com/videos/the-way-of-the-exile/.
Green, James. *The Devil Is Here in These Hills: West Virginia's Coal Miners and Their Battle for Freedom*. New York: Atlantic Monthly, 2015.
Lewis, C. S. *The Last Battle*. New York: Scholastic Inc., 1995.
———. *Mere Christianity*. New York: HarperCollins, 2001.
———. *The Screwtape Letters*. New York: HarperCollins, 2001.
Tennyson, Alfred, Lord. *In Memoriam A. H. H.* Suzeteo Enterprises, 2019.
Zaleski, Philip, and Carol Zaleski. *The Fellowship: The Literary Lives of the Inklings—J. R. R. Tolkien, C. S. Lewis, Owen Barfield, Charles Williams*. New York: Farrar, Straus, and Giroux, 2016.

www.ingramcontent.com/pod-product-compliance
Lightning Source LLC
Chambersburg PA
CBHW061512040426
42450CB00008B/1575